D1156206

# PLANES, TRAINS, AND AUTOMOBILES

## SELECTIONS FROM THE JEAN S. AND FREDERIC A. SHARF COLLECTION

MEGHAN MELVIN ········ BEN WEISS ········ NONIE GADSDEN

ISBN-10: 0-9903152-4-X
ISBN-13: 978-0-9903152-4-7

Library of Congress Control Number:
A catalog record for this book is available from the Library of Congress.

FIRST EDITION

Printed in the United States of America

This publication is to accompany the exhibit **Planes, Trains, and Automobiles: Selections from the Jean S. and Frederic A. Sharf Collection**; November 15, 2014-May 10, 2015, The Edward and Nancy Roberts Family Gallery, Museum of Fine Arts, Boston and the Norton Museum of Art, West Palm Beach Florida, Summer-Fall 2015.

The following illustrations in this book were photographed by the **Imaging Studios, Museum of Fine Arts, Boston**: cover, 4 , 6, 7, 26, 28, 30, 31, 36, 40, 41, 44, 45, 52, 53, 54, 60, 61.

Raymond Lowey illustrations pages 33-35 by photographed by **Hampton Wayt**.

All other illustrations were photographed by **Mark Wallison**, Philadelphia, PA.

**Chelsea Garunay** was the exhibition designer for the Museum of Fine Arts, Boston.

All exhibition objects are either from the private collection of Jean S. and Frederic A. Sharf, or were gifts of Jean S. and Frederic A. Sharf to the Museum of Fine Arts, Boston, with the following exception: 2014.1215 (p. 55) and 2014.1210 (p. 59), gift of Theodore W. Pietsch and family, made possible with the generous assistance of Jean S. and Frederic A. Sharf.

# CONTENTS

INTRODUCTION:

Page 5 PLANES, TRAINS, AND AUTOMOBILES

Page 7 FROM THE CURATORS

Page 9 PLANES

Page 29 TRAINS

Page 37 AUTOMOBILES

right:

**Hiller Comet spindizzy race car**
United States (San Francisco), designed 1941

Made by **Hiller Industries**, (active early 20th century

Painted metal, rubber

opposite:

**Space Shuttle Concept Model**
American, about 1972

Plastic, metal, wood

BURLINGTON

2

# PLANES, TRAINS, AND AUTOMOBILES

**Models at work**
A see-through Constellation airplane model (and a solid one) in a New York travel agent's window, about 1955.

Visitors to the Museum of Fine Arts, Boston, who read the small print have long been familiar with the names of Jean and Fred Sharf. As donors, they have appeared on hundreds of the labels next to artworks in the MFA's galleries. And what a range of works! Japanese prints, folk art, fashion design, architectural renderings, and concept drawings for automobiles, to name just a few. Fred and Jean have never had conventional taste, and have always followed their passion. In the process, they've blazed paths that many other collectors and museums have followed.

Despite that range, one theme does run through the Sharfs' collection: transportation. Planes, trains, and, most of all, automobiles appear over and over again, reflecting Fred's long fascination with the mid- 20th century's great speeding up of life. The works here capture the myriad ways designers responded to the demands of manufacturers, marketers, and even the laws of physics—and how they then gave style and snap to the simple act of getting from one place to another. There are famous names here and works by completely unidentified artists, but all capture a moment when travel had a bit more romance than it seems to possess today.

**What are models for?**

Models serve an astonishing range of purposes, and the Sharf collection includes samples of nearly every sort of miniature vehicle made during the twentieth century. There are models intended to be used in wind tunnels or to test out color schemes; models that served as prototypes, helped designers decide about shapes, or convinced companies to buy a product. Some of the models in this book were given away as trophies or sat on executives' desks; a number lured customers into travel agencies. And there are even a few toys—though just a few.

ALEXIS V. LAPTEFF
DESIGNER
37-15 72ND STR. JACKSON HGHTS.
NEW YORK, N. Y.

July 1949
SKETCH # X-10

# FROM THE CURATORS

What you see in this publication is just a tiny piece of Jean and Fred Sharf's transportation collection—literally the tip of the iceberg. So deciding what to include was a major challenge. Since we wanted to capture the collection's full range, we included some works by famous designers, some that have great stories, and a few that just looked cool. But we also wanted to capture, at least in part, the experience of being in the Sharfs' home. For it's an amazing place, where everywhere—quite literally everywhere—there are fascinating things to look at. There are paintings and folk art upstairs, architectural renderings in hallways, and shelf upon shelf of cars. In recent years, a model air force has settled onto tables and counters and nearly every other flat surface. This book and related exhibition attempt to capture that world of wonder.

**Ben Weiss**
Department Chair, Prints, Drawings and Photographs
Leonard A. Lauder Curator of Visual Culture

**Meghan Melvin**
Jean S. and Frederic A. Sharf Curator of Design

**Nonie Gadsden**
Katharine Lane Weems Senior Curator of American Decorative Arts and Sculpture

**Frederic A. Sharf**
Honorary Trustee and Millennial Benefactor

opposite:

**Alexis V. Lapteff**
American, 1905 - 1991

**Proposal for a service station**, 1949

Opaque watercolor, pastel

right:

View of the airplane model display, November 17, 2014, Edward and Nancy Roberts Family Gallery, Museum of Fine Arts, Boston

AIR FORCE

# PLANES

opposite:

**Joel F. Naprstek**
American, born in 1947
For *Swank* magazine

***Robot War***, 1976
Editorial illustration;
acrylic paint on canvas

In a densely populated sky, Joel Naprstek presents an array of aircraft from an imagined future. He made this painting in 1975 as an illustration for a prescient magazine article about the air force to come: laser-guided missiles, unmanned aircraft, and remote-controlled armed drones. Mr. Naprstek is now one of the designers of balloons and floats for the Macy's Thanksgiving Day Parade.

The Wright brothers made their famous flight in 1903, but commercial aviation didn't really begin for another two decades. After World War I brought great improvements to airplane design, the early 1920s saw the shaky beginnings of scheduled air service. By the mid-1930s, regular flights crisscrossed the United States, though flying was still mostly an affair for the wealthy. (In 1930s movies, getting on a plane was a sign of wealth and importance.) Again, though, war changed things. World War II spurred huge technological advances and the beginning of a real democratization of flight.

The design of airplanes is more closely tied to function and physics than that of cars or trains. Small changes had big effects on performance and safety, which meant that designers had less freedom of action than their counterparts at auto companies and railroads. Even so, planes from each decade do seem to fit with other designs of their era. Is that because the plane designers saw with a "period eye" and made choices that fit the look of the day; or is it because the planes—the ultimate expression of modern transport—helped set the tone for those *other* designs?

**Ungarische Aeroexpress F13**
Germany (?), after 1923

After an original airplane designed by **Hugo Junkers** (German, 1859 - 1935) and manufactured by **Junkers Flugzeug- und Motorenwerke AG**

Steel, aluminum, paint

In 1923 Hungarian Aeroexpress began using the Junkers F13 for air service between Vienna and Budapest. The plane was an obvious choice, for the airline was actually owned by Junkers, which wanted to show off its revolutionary, all-metal aircraft. The planes could carry as many as eight passengers at a time! The marking H-MACA on this model suggests it represents the first of six planes used by the company (others were H-MACB, H-MACC, and so on). All were named after birds; this one was the *Häher,* or Jay.

**Carl Walter**
American, dates unknown

***Over 200 miles per hour. International Air Races St Louis October 1-2-3***, 1923

Poster, color lithograph

Air shows and races were hugely popular in the 1920s. Extraordinary advances in flight technology combined with a surplus of skilled pilots and planes following the First World War contributed to an increase in aviation showcases. Daredevil feats and high speed races, usually performed in biplanes with open cockpits, took place across the nation to rapturous crowds. In 1920 Major Albert Lambert set out to make St. Louis a center for aviation, and was instrumental in bringing the International Air Races to the city three years later. A young Charles Lindbergh flew in to attend the high profile event and stayed on to work as a flight instructor at Lambert's air field.

**Tapestry commemorating Charles Lindbergh's flight from New York to Paris on the Spirit of St. Louis**
France, about 1927

Cotton tapestry

Charles Lindbergh's first solo non-stop flight from New York to Paris sparked an international frenzy for the young pilot and his remarkable feat of aviation. Mobbed by crowds wherever he went, savvy entrepreneurs quickly developed a wide range of commemorative souvenirs such as this tapestry.

**1930 Goodyear Zeppelin Race trophy**
United States, 1930
Made by **Medallic Art Company**

Painted white metal and painted wood base

This elegant trophy illustrates "The Evolution of Transportation" and features horse-drawn carriages, steamships, locomotives, automobiles, and the Goodyear Zeppelin above all. Zeppelins were a popular airship in the early decades of the 20th century. New York's Empire State Building was originally designed to serve as a mooring mast for zeppelins, although that dream was never realized.

**Deutsche Lufthansa Ju 52**
Germany (?), 1930s?

After an original airplane built by **Junkers Flugzeug- und Motorenwerke AG**

Cast metal

During the 1920s and early 1930s, Junkers was one of the world's leading aircraft manufacturers, and the Ju 52 among their most popular planes. It resembles, and was in many ways the primary rival to the Douglas DC-3. Introduced in 1931, Ju 52 was twice as big as the F13 (see page 10), carrying 16 passengers for 500 miles at about 150 mph. The Ju 52 was used in many countries, but it became closely associated with the Nazi party after Adolf Hitler's rise to power in 1933, when it became more or less the official airplane of the party elite.

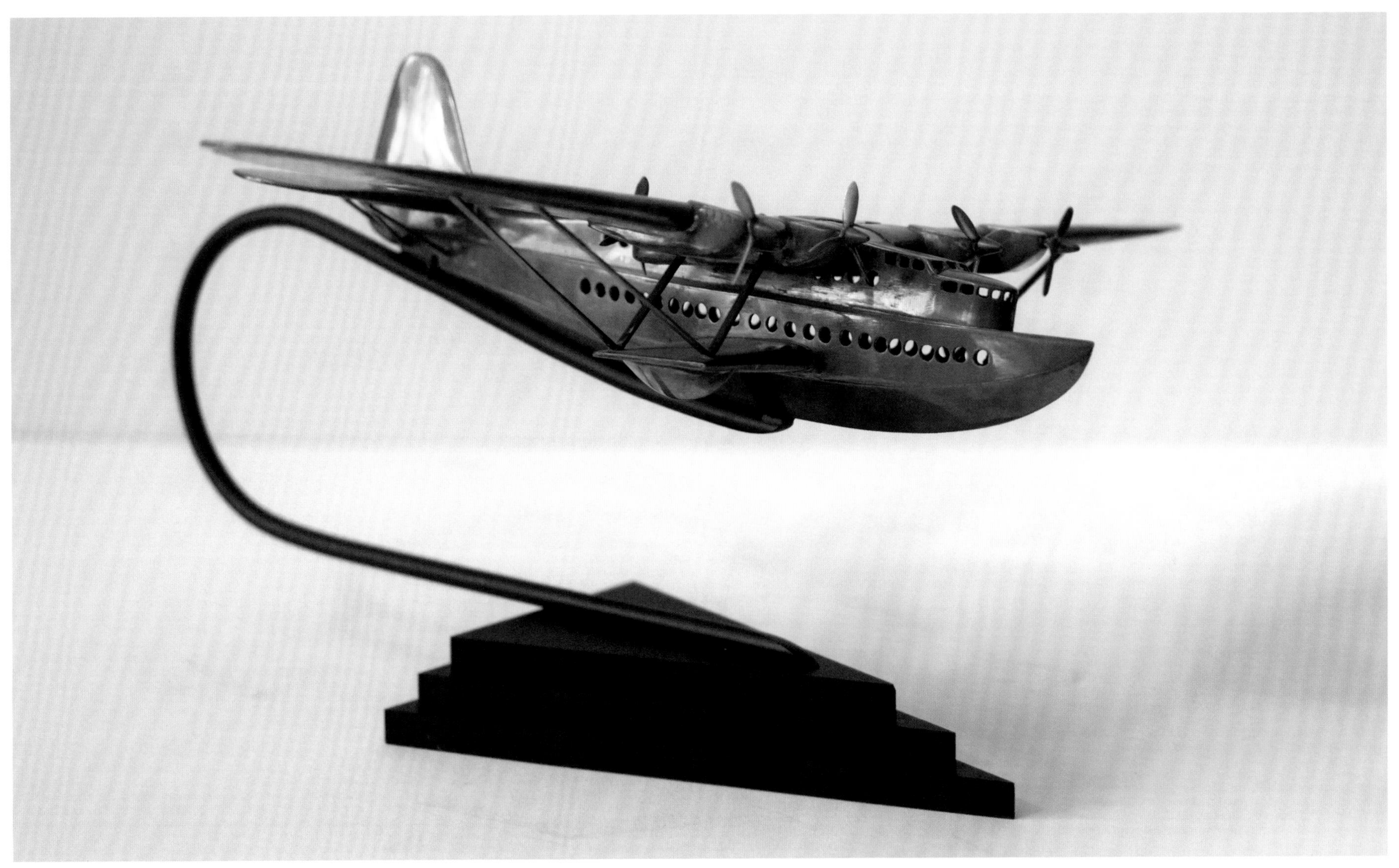

**Latécoère 521**
France (?), after 1935

Copper over aluminum or steel

This model looks like a fantasy from a 1930s children's book, but it represents an actual plane: the giant Latécoère 521 flying boat. In the 1920s and 30s, when airports were not as fully developed as they later became, planes that could land on water were quite common. The Latécoère 521 was intended as a luxury liner for the air, with private bedrooms and baths; it could fly nonstop across the Atlantic—but only one was ever built.

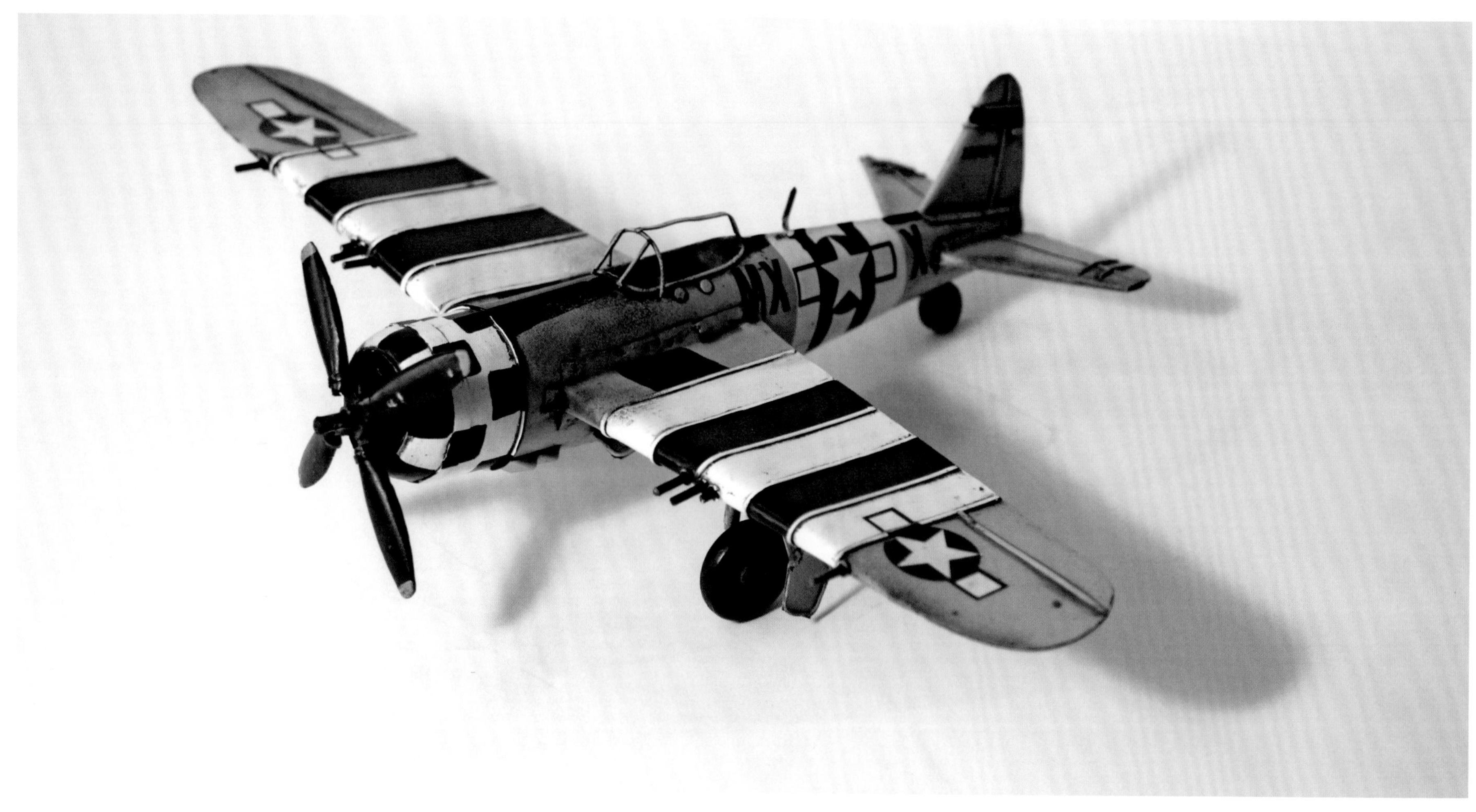

**Republic P-47 Thunderbolt**
American, 1940

Painted metal

Fighter planes were akin to the aerial infantry of World War II. They were produced by the tens of thousands, and came in many different makes and models. This model most closely resembles a P-47 Thunderbolt, which first flew in mid-1941, a few months before the United States entered the war. By the end of 1942 American and allied air forces were using it in nearly every theatre of the war. It was one of the fastest and most powerful of World War II's fighter-bombers, achieving speeds of well over 400 mph.

**Douglas C-54 Skymaster**
American, after 1943

Metal, wood

Military planes often had their roots in civilian aviation, and vice versa. The Douglas C-54 Skymaster began life as the DC-4, the Douglas Aircraft Corporation's replacement for their workhorse DC-3. It was introduced just before the beginning of World War II, and the company quickly retooled it for the war effort. The planes carried everything from soldiers to food to weapons. The model on this page commemorates the Skymasters' most public role, as the linchpin of the aerial supply chain that carried load after load of food and supplies to Berlin during the Soviet blockade of the city in 1948 and 1949.

**Douglas C-54 Skymaster**
American, after 1943

Metal, wood

**Spitfire**
English, 1944

Metal, wood

This model commemorates close cooperation between allies during World War II. Although Poland had been conquered and occupied by Nazi Germany, Poles still fought for their country's freedom after the conquest, regrouping in the United Kingdom to form an army and air force in exile. By the end of the war, there were nearly 20,000 Poles serving in the Royal Air Force and its exiled Polish counterpart. This model was presented by some of the Polish airmen on August 11, 1944 "In Remembrance of Hospitality."

**Northrop YB (or XB)-35 Flying Wing**
United States (probably Hawthorne, California), about 1946

After an original airplane designed by **Jack Northrop** (American, 1895 - 1981) and built by the **Northrop Corporation**

Painted wood and plaster

World War II provided an unparalleled opportunity for engineers and inventors to gain attention and funding for new ideas. Jack Northrop had been playing around with the idea of a flying wing since the 1920s, but only during the war did he get funding to build a prototype. The plane was designed as a very long-range bomber, and Northrop built several for testing. Technical difficulties and the advent of jet planes doomed the project, which was canceled in 1949.

**Pan American Airways Stratocruiser**
Probably United States, about 1948 - 58

After an original airplane manufactured by the **Boeing Company**

Painted metal

Names matter. Boeing called its first postwar airliner the Stratocruiser to suggest that it flew high in the stratosphere, where the air is smooth. PanAm followed suit, badging each of its planes a "clipper" to suggest speed and evoke the adventurous days of 19th-century sailing ships. The Stratocruiser helped make PanAm's Latin American and Pacific routes a big success. Look for the scuffed markings that advertise PanAir do Brasil on this model's base; it probably graced a travel agent's window somewhere in Latin America.

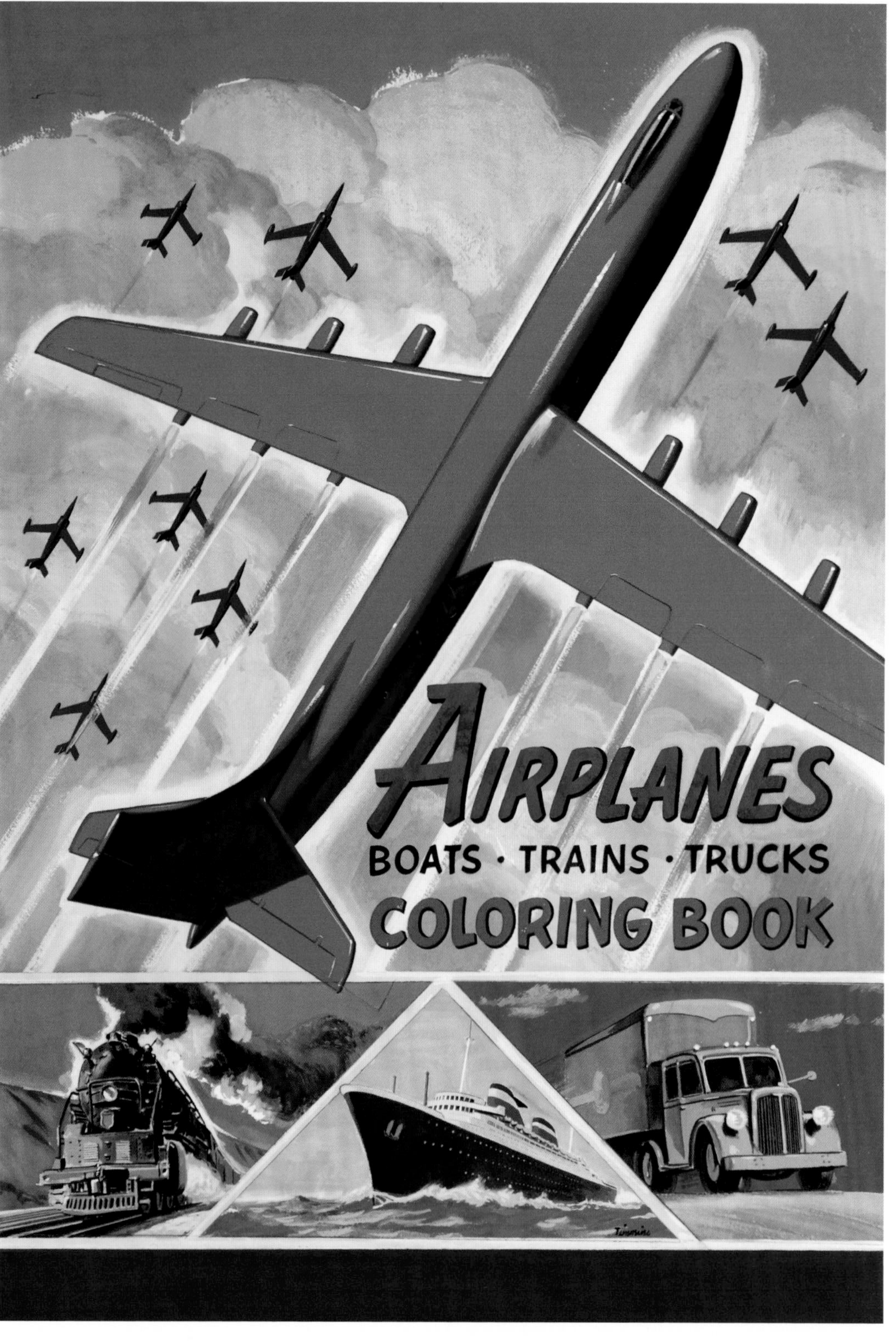


**William F. Timmins**
American, 1915 - 1985
For **The Merrill Company Publishers**

**Design for coloring book cover**, 1950

graphite, ink, opaque watercolor

**Mohawk Airlines DC-3**
United States, 1950s

After an original airplane manufactured by the **Douglas Aircraft Company**

Painted metal

The 1940s and 50s saw the growth of a number of regional airlines, which filled the void as the railroads withered. These were often low-cost companies and made much use of war-surplus planes. For example, though Mohawk advertises itself with a shiny model of its workhorse, the DC-3, the up-to-date paint job is misleading. Mohawk came into existence in 1952, but the last DC-3 came off the assembly line in 1945. This model, possibly made for the airlines president, nonetheless advertised a second-hand plane.

## THE DC-3

The DC-3 was the single most common airplane at mid-century. First introduced in 1936, the plane's bulbous nose and sturdy wings became ubiquitous during World War II, when Douglas factories in California and Oklahoma produced more than ten thousand C47s, the military version of the DC-3. Many of those aircraft survived the war, helping set the stage for a postwar aviation boom.

**Eastern Airlines Constellation**
United States, late 1940s

After an original airplane manufactured by the **Lockheed Corporation**

Painted metal, plastic

With its vaguely bird-like profile, the Constellation was among the most recognizable of airplanes, and was the biggest and fastest of the turboprop planes that dominated the decade before jets took over. Like many other airlines, Eastern used an existing transportation metaphor for its advertising; its "Great Silver Fleet" (written on the plane's side) echoes the U.S. Navy's Great White Fleet of the 1890s. The implication is that the airline is the new embodiment of American power and prowess.

**N.A.S.A. STOL Concept Plane**
American, 1950s/1960s

Plastic, metal, wood

As the military became more and more dependent on air travel in the middle of the 20th century, the problem of infrastructure began to loom very large. Bigger planes require longer runways, but wars do not always take place in areas with well developed airports. In response, engineers began to experiment with planes with that could take off at very steep angles. This concept model for a STOL or "Short Take-off and Landing" plane has wings that pivot, allowing the plane to take-off almost like a helicopter.

**Child's kimono and vest**
Japan, about 1954

Printed rayon plain weave lined with cotton plain weave

Planes, automobiles, puppies, and penguins? Even though this kimono was made for the Japanese market, the whimsical design celebrates modern American transportation including a 1954 Buick and Stratocruiser airplane. (see p.21)

opposite:

**Larry Salk**
American, 1936 - 2004

**Executives disembarking from a Beechcraft Model 33 Debonair**, 1961

Advertising proposal; graphite, opaque watercolor

This piece was drawn under the supervision of Harvey Thompson, the head of the Advertising Design Department at Art Center School, Los Angeles. Salk demonstrates his ability to incorporate product promotion into an eye-catching advertising design. Successful, stylish businessmen, carrying the latest Samsonite attaché cases, are depicted disembarking from a Beechcraft Model 33 Debonair single-engine private aircraft. All the details are very accurately rendered – the latest in narrow lapel men's suits; the appearance of the newest Beechcraft plane; the recessed hardware of the Samsonite Classic Attaché (part of a collection which was introduced in 1958 specifically for jet-age travel). Salk was a keen observer of contemporary American life.

BURLINGTON
Burlington Route

# TRAINS

At the dawn of the 20th century, American railways were at the top of their game. Manufacturers developed ever faster and more powerful locomotives; ridership was high; and trains were the essential means of getting people and goods from one place to another. The Pennsylvania Railroad's Clocker left New York for Philadelphia every hour on the hour, zipping along at nearly 100 mph for part of the trip. Long-distance trains were slower but could be quite luxurious.

But there were perils ahead. Competition from automobiles and airplanes hinted at a future when trains would no longer play the dominant role in passenger transport they had enjoyed for nearly a century. Sensing the threat, in the 1930s the railroads embraced design. Locomotives, which had always proudly worn their workings for all to see, were now dressed in sleek skins that made them seem to be moving fast even when they were standing still. Nationally recognized industrial designer Raymond Loewy, whose work is featured here, even helped the "Pennsy" dress up its dowdy old railcars and ticket booths in new clothes. But it was all for naught. By 1960 the planes and cars had won, and although freight transportation continues strong to this day the passenger railroads entered the long, slow decline from which they've never really recovered.

opposite, pages 30 - 31

**Burlington Zephyr electric train model**
Made by Western Coil and Electric Company
after the original train manufactured by
Edward G. Budd Manufacturing Company
Designed 1934, made 1934 - 40
Cast aluminum, plastic, electrical components

A modern marvel of both engineering and streamlined style, the Burlington Zephyr was unveiled to great publicity and fanfare with its record-breaking "Dawn-to-Dusk" run from Denver to Chicago on May 26, 1934. Made of lighter weight materials (such as stainless steel) and powered by an efficient and reliable new diesel engine, the Zephyr caught the public's attention with its sleek, aerodynamic design. The *New York Times* credited the Zephyr with "ushering in a new era in railroad history." This model was constructed simultaneously with the full-sized train, from the original Zephyr plans provided by the manufacturer. The model makers tried to keep up with last-minute production changes to the locomotive, but some elements vary slightly from the train's final design.

BURLINGTON-ZEPHYR
9900

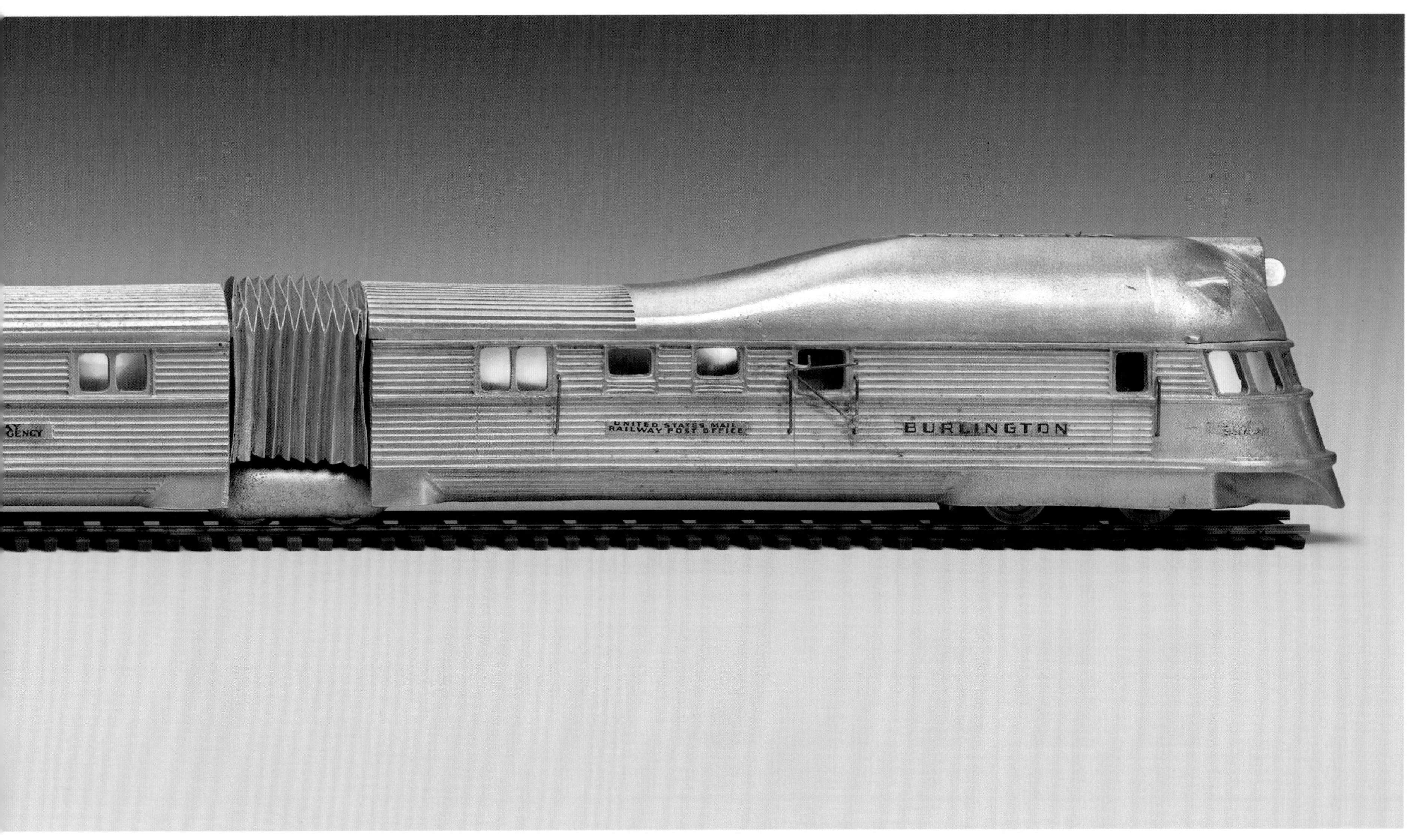
UNITED STATES MAIL
RAILWAY POST OFFICE
BURLINGTON

**Raymond Loewy**
American (born in France), 1893 - 1986

***Vacationland via Pennsylvania R.R.***, about 1939

Opaque and transparent watercolor with metallic paint, over graphite

The Pennsylvania Railroad, at one point the nation's largest rail company, was one of Raymond Loewy's most significant clients. Here Loewy transforms a simple ticket booth—very likely Penn Station around the time of the New York World's Fair—into an alluring advertisement for long-distance train travel out West.

**Raymond Loewy**
American (born in France), 1893 - 1986

**Long Island Railroad double-deck cars color scheme**, about 1946

Graphite, opaque watercolor, crayon

The following selection of designs (pp. 33-35) reflects new thinking about the experience of travel for commuters and tourists alike. Loewy's schemes reflect his dedication to improving modern life through his principle of "most advanced yet acceptable" design. From an elegant cocktail bar to a playroom, all of the travelers' needs are addressed in style.

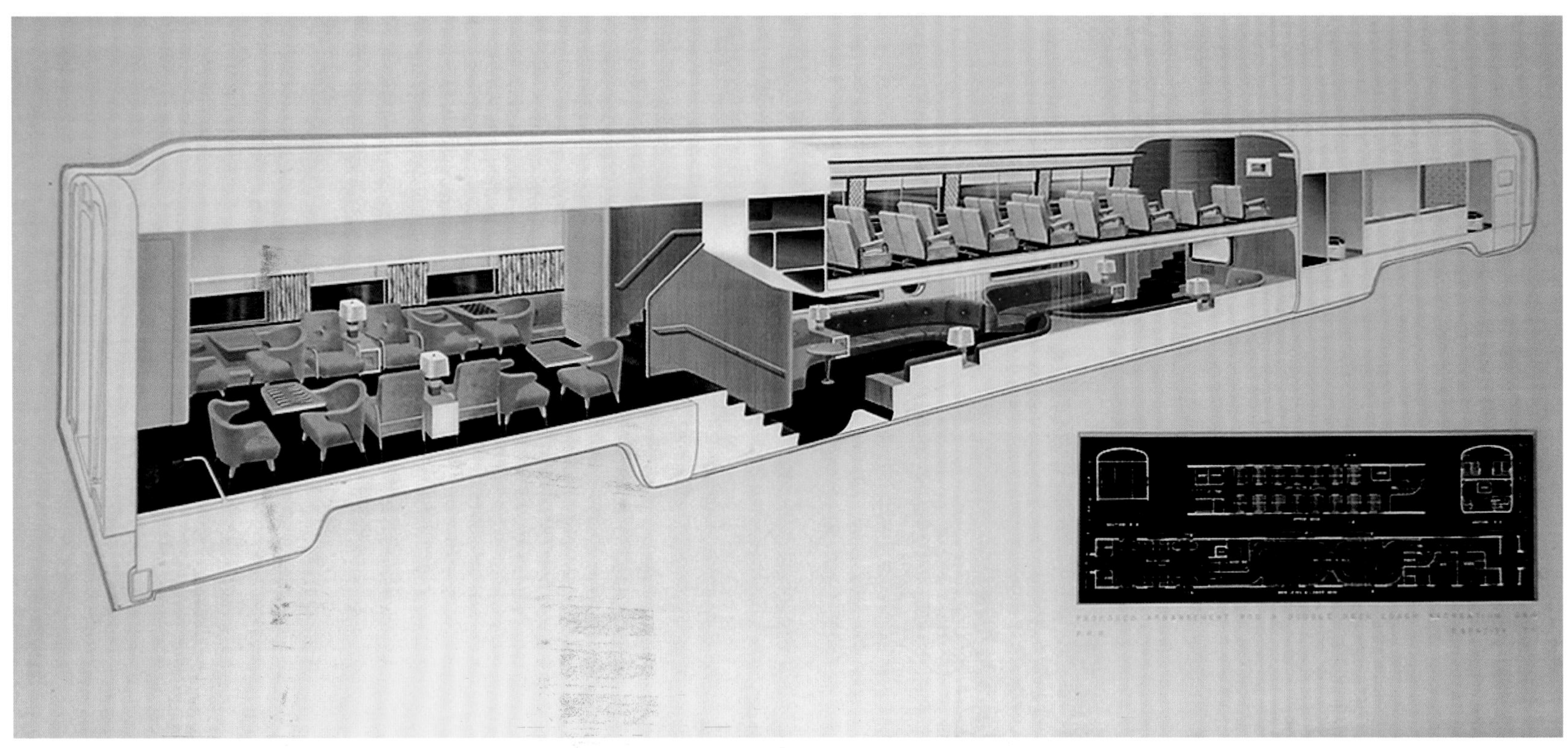

**Raymond Loewy**
American (born in France), 1893 - 1986

**Proposed arrangement for a doubledeck coach recreation car–Pennsylvania Railroad**, 1947

Graphite, opaque watercolor, gelatin silver photograph

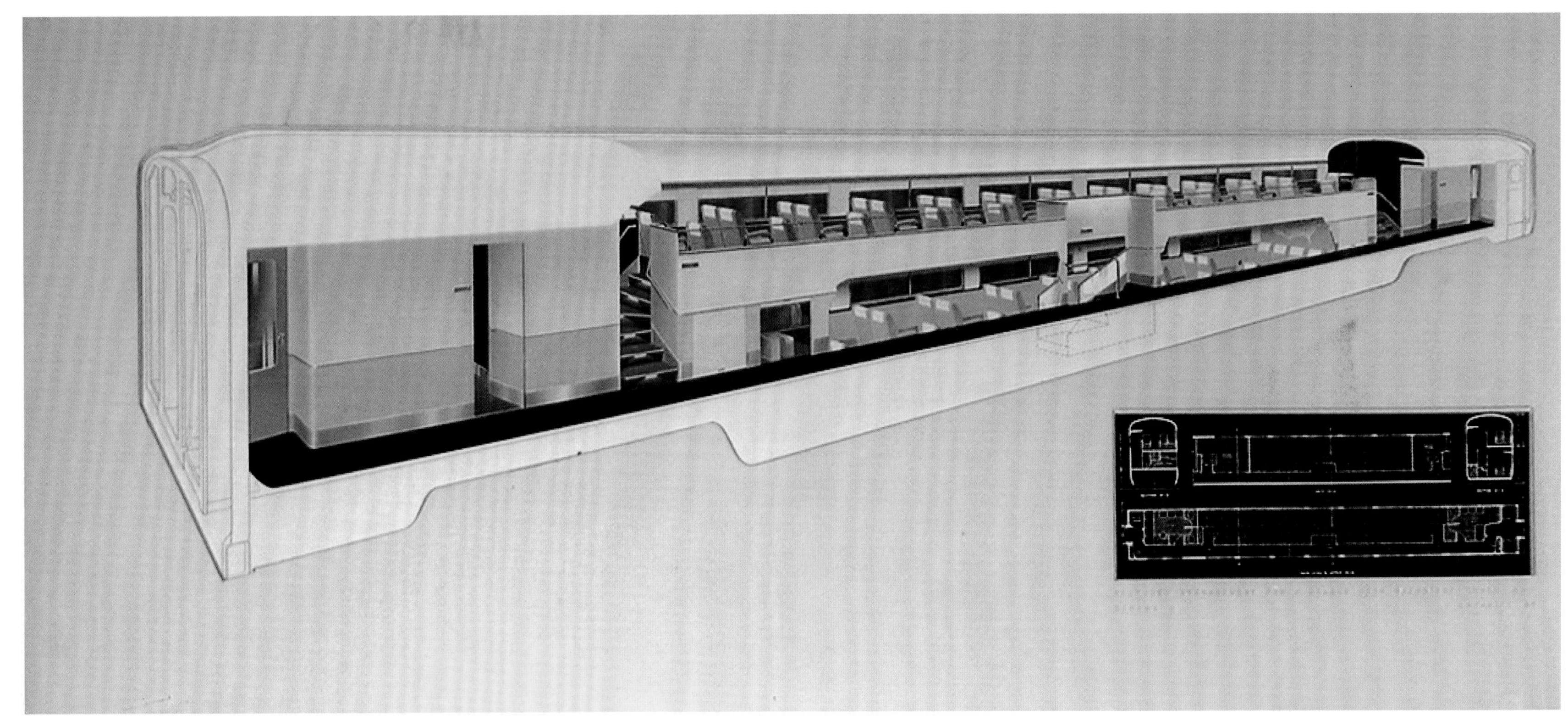

**Raymond Loewy**
American (born in France), 1893 - 1986

**Proposed arrangement for a doubledeck overnight coach–Pennsylvania Railroad, Scheme 2**, 1947

Graphite, opaque watercolor, metallic paint, gelatin silver photograph

H.C. LaGassey, Jr.

# AUTOMOBILES

The age of automotive styling officially began in 1927, when General Motors president Alfred P. Sloan, Jr. hired Harley J. Earl to add "eye appeal" to car design. Until then, for the first three decades after the invention of the modern automobile, car manufacturers had paid little attention to the aesthetic appearance of their products. Dependability, durability and cost were their top concerns. GM's Sloan believed that the emotional appeal of attractive styling and yearly model changes could help his company successfully compete with Henry Ford's ubiquitous Model T. He was right.

Before long, car design was a dominant force in the manufacture and sales of American automobiles. As GM's Public Relations department dramatically declared in 1958: "This dynamic obsolescence caused by the annual model change is the life-blood of the auto industry and a key factor in the national economy."

This collection of automotive art and design loosely represents the evolution of car styling in the United States from the 1920s to the early 1970s through design drawings, models, promotional materials, competition entries, toys, related automobile culture, and more.

**Homer C. LaGassey**
American, 1924 - 2014

**Concept for a two-door sedan,** about 1946

Colored crayon, opaque watercolor

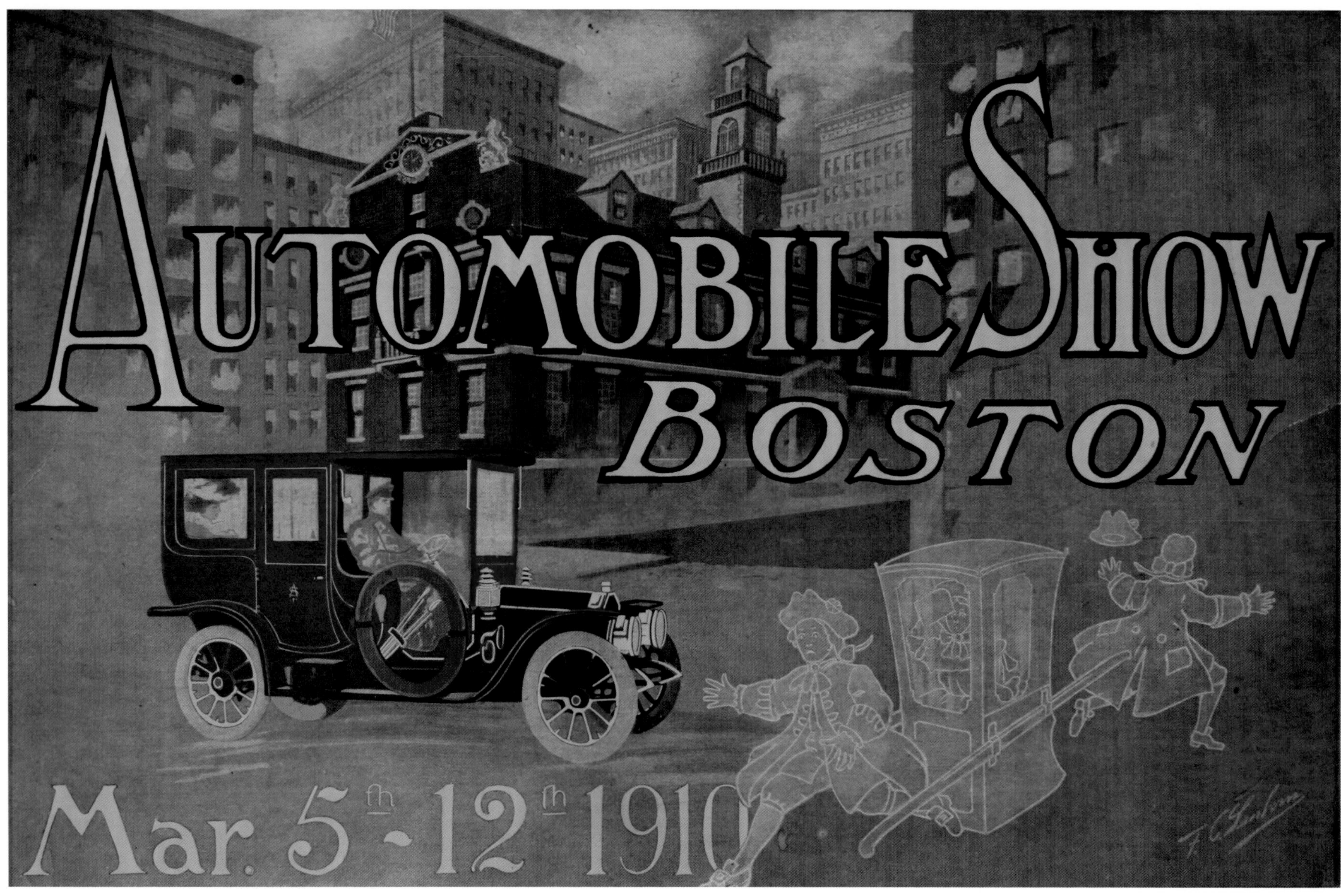


**F.C. Sanborn**
American, dates unknown

**Automobile Show Boston**
**Mar 5th - 12th 1910, 1910**

Poster, color lithograph

**Clarence Peter Helck**
American, 1893 - 1988

**Illustration for a Model 48 *Locomobile* advertisement**, 1919

Graphite, ink, crayon, opaque watercolor

This advertising illustration of a stylish young woman making her way through the snow to the haven of a *Locomobile* sedan was created when the manufacturer was at the height of their popularity. In 1917 General "Black Jack" Pershing, the newly appointed leader of the American Expeditionary Forces (A.E.F.) overseas, sought out reliable vehicles for use by himself and other senior officers. The Locomobile Company of America was selected to supply these vehicles, including a sedan customized for Pershing. He continued to use a *Locomobile* upon his return to the United States; Pershing's highly publicized use of the luxury car no doubt contributed to the firm's success well into the 1920s.

**Kissel engineering/styling car model**
United States (Hartford, Wisconsin), about 1920

Designed and made by **J. Friedrich Werner** (American, born in Germany) for **Kissel Motor Car Company**

Maple, ash, and other woods

From 1906 to 1931, the Kissel Motor Car Company made custom-built automobiles with wooden frames clad in pressed steel. Designs for cars during this period slowly transformed from open-air, high, carriage-like bodies to closed sedans with lower centers of gravity. This maple design and engineering model for a seven passenger closed touring car dates to about 1920.

**Darwin Blake Battles**
American, 1888 - 1972

**Cord L-29,** about 1930

Graphite, opaque watercolor

**Golden Arrow model car**
United States, about 1929

Cast metal, paint, painted plaster

British major Henry Seagrave broke the international Land Speed Record on March 11, 1929 when his Golden Arrow reached 231.446 mph at Daytona Beach, Florida. The Golden Arrow's sleek body made of lightweight aluminum sheeting was designed by Captain J.S. Irving and manufactured by Thrupp & Maberly. This model was made simultaneously with the full-sized vehicle and probably presented as a gift to one of Seagrave's financial backers. An identical model that is said to have been used as a wind-tunnel test model was given by J.S. Irving to the Institution of Mechanical Engineers in London in the late 1930s.

**Speed of the Wind wind tunnel model**
England, about 1935

Painted pine

Designed by Englishmen Captain George Eyston and E.A.D. Eldridge, the Speed of the Wind broke speed endurance records in 1935 when it averaged 140.52 mph over a 24-hour period. This painted pine model, created during the design process, was used in wind tunnel tests. The opposite side bears handwritten scientific annotations about the aerodynamic properties of this shape.

**1934 LaSalle design model**
United States (Detroit), about 1933

Designed and made by **Harley J. Earl** (American, 1893 - 1969) for **General Motors Corporation**

Mahogany, painted black, chrome-plated metal, glass

Harley J. Earl, a carriage maker's son who had worked in a custom body shop in Los Angeles, brought the glitz and glam of his Hollywood clientele to Detroit to establish the industry's first automotive design division, General Motors' "Art and Colour Department." His first complete car design, the sleek 1927 La Salle (a predecessor to the 1934 La Salle model seen here) was an immediate success, prompting other car companies to take notice and develop styling departments of their own.

**Airomobile prototype model**
United States (Denver), 1936

Designed by **Paul M. Lewis** (American, died in 1990) and **John Tjaarda** (American, born in the Netherlands, 1897 - 1962)
Manufactured by **McPherson Foundry**

Painted cast aluminum, polished aluminum

In 1933, dreamer and inventor Paul M. Lewis conceived of the Airomobile, a three-wheeled, aerodynamic and affordable family car. He worked with automobile designer John Tjaarda to create a small series of 1/10 scale, sand-cast prototypes, which he used to attract investors in his endeavor. This model is believed to be one of those early prototypes. After several technical difficulties were conquered, a full-size experimental model was created in 1937, which Lewis drove on a promotional tour throughout the United States. Although the teardrop-shaped, three-wheeled car attracted much attention, concerns about its stability and handling, along with the advent of WWII, kept it from ever going into full production.

**Car model for Fisher Body Craftsman's Guild competition**
United States (Pasadena, California), 1937

Made by **Edgar C. Outten Jr.**
(American, 1921 - 2000)

Painted pine, metal, miniature light bulbs

The Fisher Body Company, a leading early manufacturer of auto bodies, was acquired by General Motors at the start of the 1920s. With the onset of the Depression, the Fishers wanted to give back. They organized a philanthropic foundation, "an organization for the development of craftsmanship and creative ability among boys," called the Fisher Body Craftsman's Guild in 1930. The Guild held annual auto design competitions for young men aged 12 to 19 from 1931 until 1968, awarding millions over the years in scholarship funds. This example, made by a young Edgar C. Outten, Jr. of Pasadena, California in 1937, was created for the first year in which contestants were given the opportunity to design their own cars.

opposite:

**Welch and Trumpfheller**
American, dates unknown

**Cadillac Series 65 (Custom V8) and Series 75 (Fleetwood) Egg Crate Front Grill Design: Model Year 1938,** 1937

Graphite, opaque watercolor

**Alexis V. Lapteff**
American, 1905 - 1991

**Mercury Four-Door Town Sedan, model year 1939**, 1938

Graphite, opaque watercolor

Ford Motor Company introduced the Mercury Eight in 1939 and featured it prominently in "The Road of Tomorrow", their massive exhibit at the New York World's Fair. Promoted as a large, high-quality car "that truly dares to ask 'Why?'", the Mercury was an immediate commercial success for Ford.

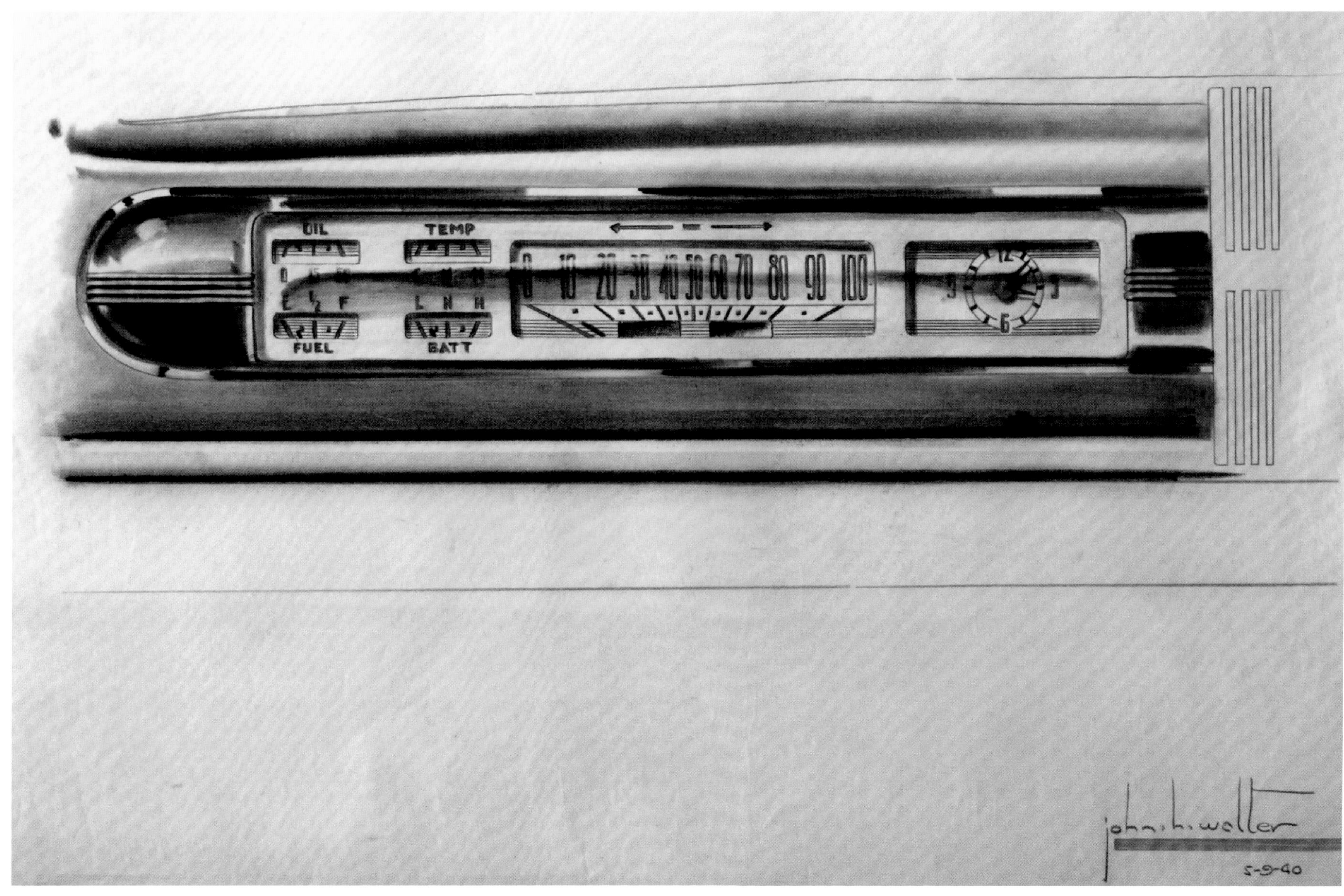


**John H. Walter**
American, dates unknown
For **Ford Motor Company**

**Proposal for an instrument cluster and radio**, 1940

Graphite, colored crayon

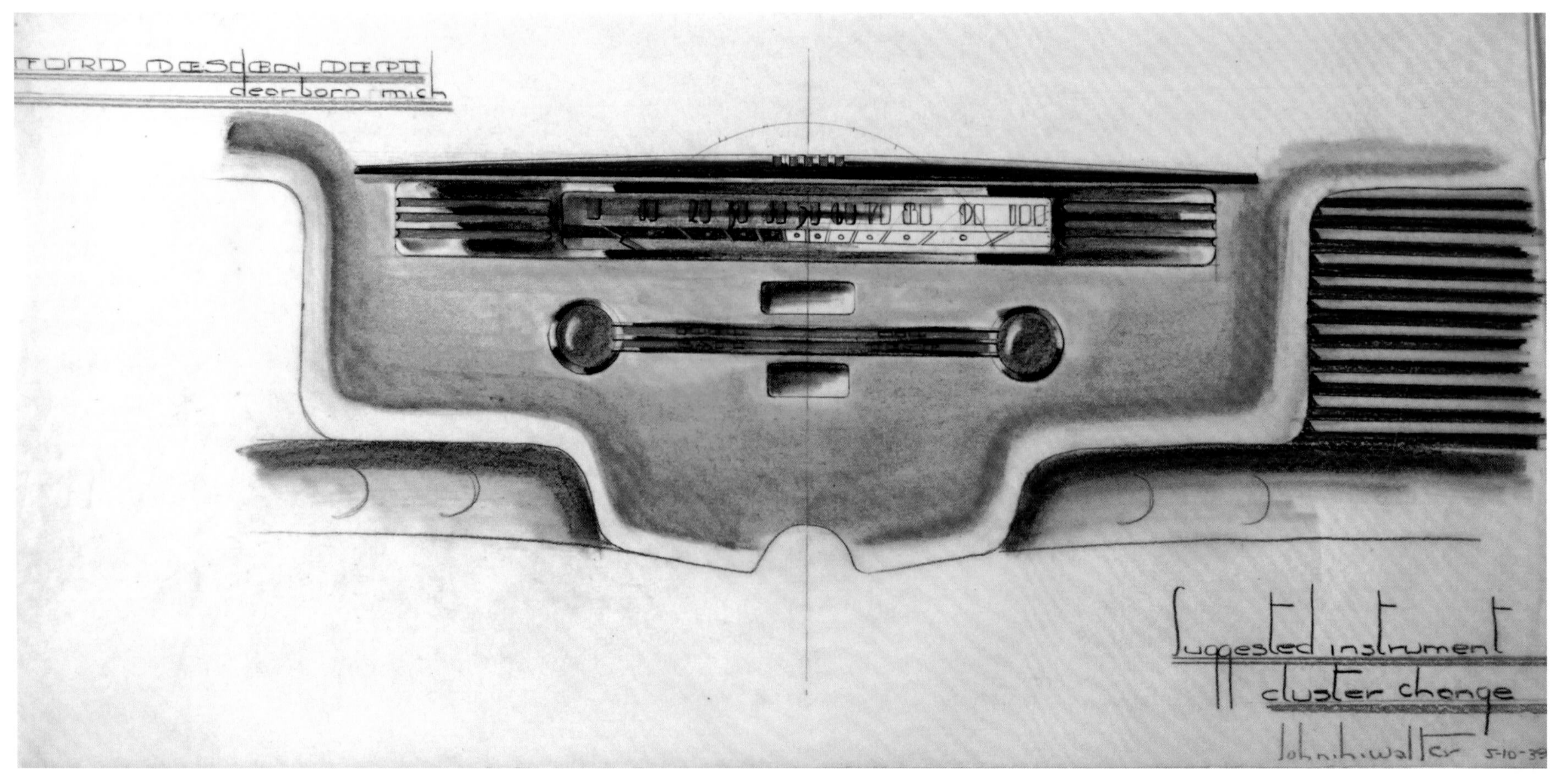


**John H. Walter**
American, dates unknown
For **Ford Motor Company**

**Suggested instrument cluster change,** 1939

Graphite, colored crayon

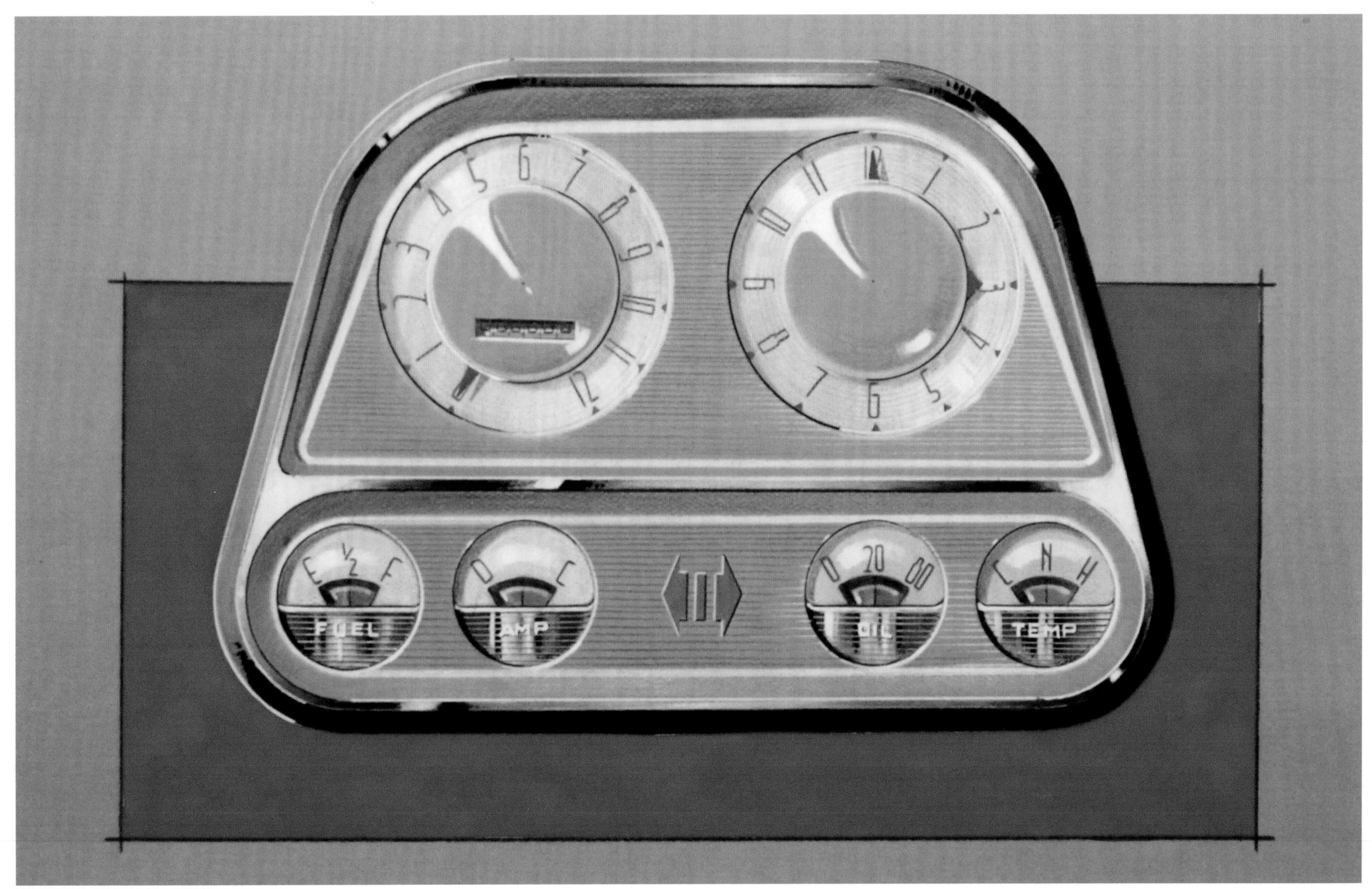


**William M. Schmidt Associates**
American, active 1959 - 2005

**Proposal for an instrument gauge cluster**, about 1960

Graphite, opaque watercolor, colored crayon

**Mercury Deluxe spindizzy racer**
United States (Los Angeles, California), designed 1939

Manufactured by **Dooling Brothers**

Painted cast aluminum, sheet aluminum, rubber, leather, plastic

Spindizzies, or tether cars, were handbuilt model racecars popular during the late 1930s through the late 1940s. The Dooling Brothers of Los Angeles are credited with starting the fad in early 1937 when they experimented with model airplane engines to run model cars. By 1939, the craze for miniature gas-powered car racing had spread across the country. Like this Mercury Deluxe model designed by the Dooling Brothers in 1939, most spindizzies were finely crafted miniature versions of the full-sized racing cars of the era.

**Maserati spindizzy racer**
England, 1940s

Painted cast and sheet aluminum, rubber, leather, plastic

**Challenger spindizzy racer**
United States, about 1948

Manufactured by **M & E Models, Ltd**

Painted wood, sheet tin, metal, cast aluminum, rubber, leather, plastic

**Dump truck model**
United States (Cleveland), 1941

Designed by **Viktor Schreckengost** (American, 1906 - 2008) for **Steelcraft**, a division of **Murray Ohio Company**

Steel, paint, rubber

Victor Schreckengost is best known for his work in pottery, such as his iconic Art Deco "Jazz Bowl" series. However, he also had a prolific career as an industrial designer, making designs for pedal cars, bicycles, lawn mowers, and more.

**Theodore Wells Pietsch II**
American, 1912 - 1993

**Proposal for a "bathtub" sedan**, 1943

Graphite, opaque watercolor

**Willys *Jeepster* model**
United States (Toledo, Ohio), about 1947

Made by **Al-Toy**, a division of **Toledo Casting Corporation**
After original car manufactured by **Willys-Overland Motors, Inc.**

Cast aluminum, paint, plastic

Towards the end of World War II, Willys-Overland hired industrial designer Brooks Stevens to transform their successful and dependable military Jeep into a commercial, civilian vehicle. Steven's utilitarian, yet stylish Jeep Station Wagon was released in 1946, followed two years later by the convertible Jeepster luxury touring car. Company executives celebrated the success of these vehicles by teaming with Al-Toy to create highly detailed models to use as Christmas gifts and rewards to salesmen. The Jeepster model was released at the end of 1947, while the Station Wagon model dates from Christmas 1948.

**Willys Jeep Station Wagon model**
United States (Toledo, Ohio), about 1948

Made by **Al-Toy**, a division of **Toledo Casting Corporation**
After original car designed by Brooks Stevens
(American, 1911 - 1995) for **Willys-Overland Motors, Inc.**

Cast aluminum, paint, plastic

**Richard Arbib**
American, 1917 - 1995

**Proposal for a two-door convertible, model year 1950**, 1950

Graphite, opaque watercolor

**Theodore Wells Pietsch II**
American, 1912 - 1993

**For Ford Motor Company, proposal for Meteor sedan**, about 1950

Graphite, opaque watercolor

**Greyhound Scenicruiser bus model**
United States, mid 1950s

Made by **General Motors Corporation**
After original bus designed by **Raymond Loewy**
(American, born in France, 1893 - 1986)

Painted plaster, printed decals, wood

Featuring air-conditioning, comfortable seating, a complete washroom, a double-deck interior, and its signature panoramic windows, the Greyhound Scenicrusier was touted in period advertisements as "revolutionary" and "setting standards of travel luxury and sightseeing pleasure never before offered to motor bus passengers." Put into service in 1954, Scenicrusier was the result of a ten-year collaboration between Greyhound, General Motors, and industrial designers Raymond Loewy and Associates. Loewy and his staff were responsible for design of the sleek, streamlined exterior as well as the comfortable, passenger-friendly interior. This four-foot long plaster model was used as a promotional tool in Greyhound terminals across the country.

**1955 Lincoln Futura model car**
United States (Gum Springs, Virginia),
designed 1955; made about 1994

Made by **Marty Martino** (American)
After original car designed by **William M. Schmidt** (American, born about 1916) and **John Najjar Ferzely** (American, 1918 - 2011) for **Ford Motor Company**

Fiberglas, wood, plastic, rubber, paint

Bill Schmidt, chief stylist at the Ford Motor Company after World War II, claimed that he based his design for the Lincoln Futura on the mako sharks and manta rays he saw while scuba-diving in the Bahamas. Nineteen-feet long with a clear-plastic bubble canopy and outrageously exaggerated tailfins, the Futura attracted enormous attention when it was unveiled at the Chicago Auto Show in January 1955. Yet, the two-passenger car was also wildly impractical and very expensive—the prototype cost $250,000 to create—and therefore never put into production. The Futura's popularity was revived in 1966 when auto customizer George Barris modified the prototype into the first Batmobile for the new Batman television series. This limited edition model was created using the original design plans from Ford.

**Warner**
American, dates unknown

**1961 Corvette,** 1961

Graphite, opaque watercolor

**Roland J. Sigafoo**
American, 1914 - 2006

**Design for a camper van**, 1968

Graphite, pen and ink,
opaque watercolor

# BLMC ADO 71

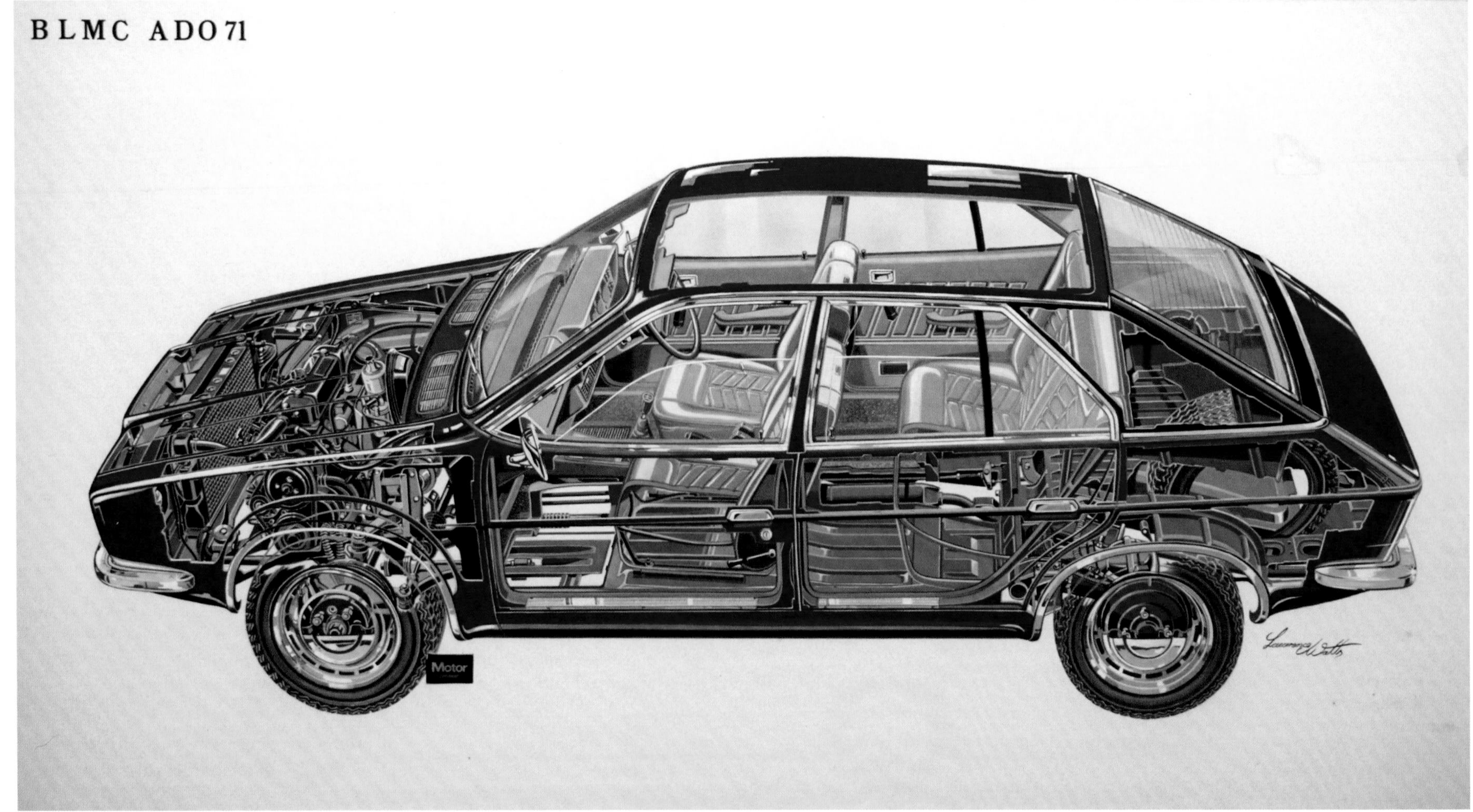


**Lawrence Watts**
English, died in 2012

**Cutaway illustration of BLMC ADO 71 for *MOTOR* magazine**, 1974

Graphite, opaque watercolor